ABC's of RUGBY LEAGUE

THIS BOOK BELONGS TO

○○○○○○○○○○○○○○○○○○○○○○○○○○○○○○○○○○

Advantage

"ADVANTAGE"

Advantage is..
Referee shouts advantage and play-on, waving their arms, chest height hands facing down. in a crossing motion

(Japan)

(Netherlands)

(Turkey)

Ball

b

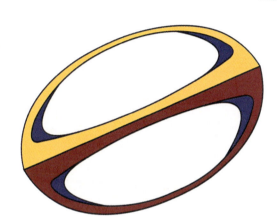

Ball is..

The main piece of equipment that is used.
The ball is an ovel shap, similar to an egg.
The ball must ALWAYS be passed backwards.

(Norway)

(Hungary)

(Ghana)

Conversion

C

Conversion is..

Kicking the ball between the post, over the crossbar.
A conversion is worth 2 points.
A conversion takes place when:
A team scores a try
A team wins a penalty and kicks the goal

(Canada)

(Denmark)

(USA)

Drop-Kick d

Drop-Kick is..

Kicking the ball from hand between the post andover the crossbar. The ball MUST bounce on the ground before kicking.
A Drop-Kick can be used as a conversion (worth 2 points) or as a Drop-Goal (worth 1 point)

(Netherlands) (Ireland) (Scotland)

Evade

Evade is..

Using fast feet to go around the defenders trying not to get tackled.

(Scotland)

(England)

(South Africa)

Full Back f

Full Back is..

A main position in the sport of Rugby League.
This player is usually a great tackler and ball catcher.
The Full-Back can usually be seen wearing jersey number 1.

(Australia)

(Wales)

(Russia)

Grubber g

Grubber is..

A type of kick that tumbles and rolls along the ground.
This kick is more difficult for defenders to catch,

(Ghana)

(Australia)

(England)

Hooker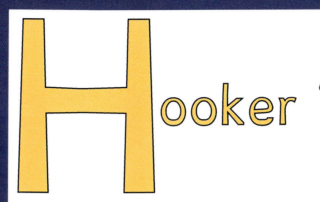

Hooker is..

A main position in the sport of Rugby League.
This player usually passes the ball out of the Paly the ball.
The Hooker can usually be seen wearing jersey number 9.

(Netherlands)   (Norway)   (Australia)

Interchange

Interchange is..

The swapping/ replacaing one player for another. Interchange is also the name givento a player who is not in the starting line-up but is a replacement.

 (Vanuatu)   (Peru)   (England)

Juggle   j

Juggle is..
Trying to control a ball whilst it is in the air.
Always try and attempt to catch the ball on the first attempt.

(Jamaica)   (Czech Republic)   (Nigeria)

Knock-on

k

Knock-on is..

Losing possession/ control of the ball and it going forward and bounces on the ground.

(England)

(Sweden)

(Ukraine)

Loose-forward

Loose-forward is..

A main position in the sport of Rugby League.
This player is usually one of the fittest members in the team.
The Loose-Forward can usually be seen wearing jersey number 13.

(USA)

(South America)

(Norway)

Marker   m

Marker is..

A defender which following the tackle stands infront of the play the ball. There should always be atleast one marker.

(Czech Republic)   (South Africa)   (Jamaica)

No High Tackle

No High-Tackle is..

Tackling a defender above the shoulders.
It is illegal to tackle a player above the shoulders.

(Russia)

(Belgium)

(Wales)

Offload

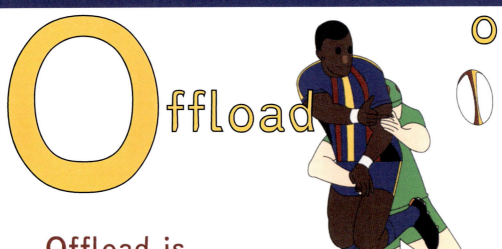

Offload is..
Passing the ball whilst being tackled by a defender.

(USA)

(Czech Republic)

(Norway)

Play-The Ball

Play - The Ball is..

After the player with the ball is tackled, they must lift the ball and roll it behind them using their foot.

(France) (Serbia) (Greece)

Quarter

Quarter is..

Unlike some other sports Rugby League is played as two 40 minute halves.
On a hot day, a game of Rugby League can be played in four, 20 minute quarters.

(Australia)

(England)

(USA)

R^{eferee r}

Referee is..

Is the person in charge of play whilst playing on the field. Referee is the only non-player on the field for the entire game.

(Serbia)

(Greece)

(Netherlands)

S crum

Scrum is..

A scrum is a method of restarting
play in Rugby League,
this involves players packing closely.
No pushing will be involved.
Scrum is short for Scrummage

(Cameroon)

(England)

(Sweden)

Up-and-Over

Up-and-Over is..

A type of kick that goes up in the air and behind/ over the the defenders.
This type of kick can also be named:
Punt, Bomb, Chip and Chase

(Australia)

(England)

(Brazil)

Voluntary tackle

Voluntary tackle is..
A player in possession shall not deliberately and unnecessarily allow themselves to be tackled by voluntarily falling to the ground when not held by an opponent

(Wales)

(Canada)

(Brazil)

Winger

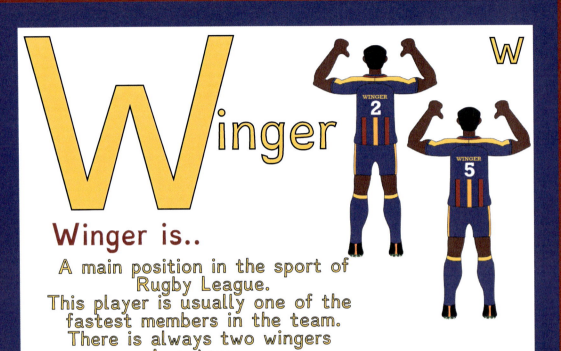

Winger is..

A main position in the sport of Rugby League.
This player is usually one of the fastest members in the team.
There is always two wingers in a team.
Wingers can usually be seen wearing jersey numbers 2 and 5.

(Poland)

(Jamaica)

(Wales)

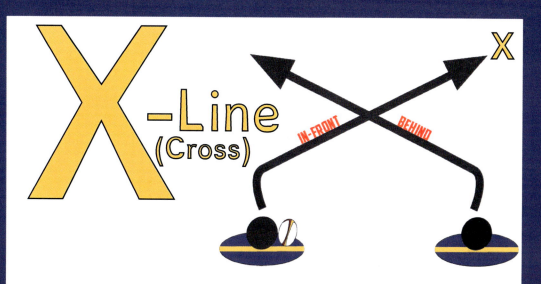

X-Line (Cross) is..

To open up gaps, players cross, and the first player passes the ball off his hip into the path of the second player using an "X line" to trick defenders

(Ireland)

(England)

(France)

Yellow card

y

Yellow card is..

A yellow card is used to signal that a player is being temporarily suspended from the game. The player is sent to the "sin bin" for 10 minutes, after which time they are allowed to return to carry on playing.

(Australia)   (England)   (Cameroon)

Zero tackle

O[z]

Zero tackle is..

If the defending team 'knocks on' or touches the ball when it's in the air, and the ball is immediately regathered by the attacking team, the referee may elect to restart the tackle count by shouting Zero or Zero tackle.

(Nigeria)

(Serbia)

(Netherlands)

RUGBY LEAGUE CLUBS

Abiko Ducks, Amsterdam Cobras, Aqua Warriors, Bastos Majestics, Brighouse Rangers, Bodø Barbarians, Budapest RL, Bulls RLFC, Capilano Cougars, Copenhagen RLFC, Cleveland, Den Haag Knights, Dublin City Exiles, Dundee Dragons, Edinburgh Eagles, Egremont Rangers, Ermelo Tamohawks, Fitrzroy Gracemere Sharks, Flintshire Falcons, Flying Dutchmen Sevastopol, Forth Valley Vikings, Ghana Skolars, Glebe Dirty Reds, Gloucester All Golds, Harderwijk Dolphins, Haugesend Sea Eagles, Hela Wigmen, Ifira Black Birds, Incas, Ince Rose, JDF Warriors, Jilemnice RL, Jos Miner, Kimbe Cutters, KR Tirana, Kungsbacka Broncos, Kyiv Rhinos, LA Mongrals, Latin Heat, Lillestrøm Lions, Mad Squirrels, Middelburg Tigers, Mona Pelicans, Nevskaya Zastava St. Petersburg, North Brussels Gorillas, North Wales Crusaders Wheelchair Rugby League, Orli Havlíčkův Brod, Orgeon, Oslo Capitals, Palau Broncos, Partizan Belgrade, Perama Tigers, Queanbeyan Blues, Queens City Royals, Queensbury ARLFC, Red Star Belgrade, Rhodes Knights, Rotterdam Pitbulls, Sahel Rugby Club XIII Garoua, Shaw Cross Sharks, Stockholm Kings, The Guyra Super Spuds, Torfaen Tigers, Trakya Gladyatorler, Trondheim, UC Stars, Underbank Rangers, Urutau, Valley Cougars, Valley Warriors, Vitoria Rhinos, Wataha Piotrków Tryb, West Kingston Hyenas, Wrexham Crusaders, X-League KTRA, X-League North Yorkshire, XIII Limouxin, Yass Minor, York Acorns, Youndé Bulls, Zazzau Bulls, Zemun XIII, Zwolle Wolves

RUGBY LEAGUE CLUBS

RUGBY LEAGUE GOVERNANCE

Ade Adebisi – Nigeria Rugby League
Albania Rugby League
Belgian Rugby League Association (Belgium)
Brasil Rugby League (Brazil)
British Columbia Rugby League – Canada Rugby League
California Rugby League (USA – LA Mongrels)
Cameroon Rugby League XIII
Czech Rugby League Association (Czech Republic)
Daan Van Rossum – Netherlandse Rugby League Bond (Netherlands)
Danmark Rugby League (Denmark)
Declan Foy – X-League – Rugby Football League (England & Ireland)
Fédération Française de Rugby à XIII (France)
Frans Erasmus & Frans Parsons – South Africa Rugby League
Gareth Kear – Wales Rugby League
Greek Rugby League Association (Greece)
Jafaru Mustapha – Rugby League Federation Ghana
Jaime Perez – Peru Rugby League XIII
John McMullen – Rugby Football League (England)
Jon Christie – Russian Association of Rugby League Clubs (Russia)
Jonatan Dam – Rugby League Norge (Norway)
Julien Treu – Turkish Rugby League Association (Turkey)
New South Wales (Australia)
Ollie Cruishank – Scotland Rugby League
Polska Rugby XIII (Poland)
Queensland Rugby League (Australia)
Romeo Monteith – Jamaica Rugby League Association
Rugby League Ireland
Sam Cammell, Sebastian Johnson-Cadwell & Fabian Wikander
Sweden Rugby League
Ukraine Rugby League
Vanuatu Rugby League

RUGBY LEAGUE GOVERNANCE

Made in the USA
Columbia, SC
24 January 2021